DEVELOP AN EFFECTIVE RESEARCH PROPOSAL

FOR THESIS, DISSERTATION, OR PROJECT

Learn the key research components, know the nuances of how to structure, communicate convincingly, and create an outstanding proposal.

DR. SUMAN MUNDKUR

The link to Your Free eBook
https://sumanmundkur.com/ebook

You can download the eBook and use it if you have to decide on your topic. If you already have selected a topic, go right on to your proposal development!

DISCLAIMER

While all attempts have been made to verify the information provided in this publication, the author does not assume any responsibility for errors, omissions, or contrary interpretations of the subject matter herein. The views expressed are those of the author alone and should not be taken as expert instruction or commands. The reader is responsible for his or her own actions. The author makes no representations or warranties with respect to the accuracy or completeness of the contents of this work and specifically disclaims all warranties, including without limitation warranties of fitness for a particular purpose.

PREFACE

Proposal writing is an art based on certain scientific principles to create a pitch on a subject. The aim is to seek approval from the evaluation team for granting admission to a Ph.D. program, a research project, or to secure research grants. There are different kinds of proposals. This book specifically covers the development of proposals effectively for academic institutions, post-graduate students, Ph.D. aspirants, graduate students who would like to take up research projects, and scholars who are looking for research funding.

Good proposals are well structured in content, concise, and convincing, intended for and leading the reader to approve. Writing a good proposal requires a significant amount of dedicated work time, clear foresight, good planning, and a well-thought process on the content, context, and layout. It also involves understanding the target audience, the reader, reviewers, and keeping the editor in mind. Unlike traditional essay writing, proposal writing is done with an intent to impress the subject of research, to persuade the reader, and convince them of the ideas presented by the researcher.

Most aspiring researchers are enthusiastic about conducting research. But they are unsure about what to include and what not to in the research

proposal or a grant proposal. Seeking grants for research is competing for limited resources, which means it needs a certain amount of skill in writing convincingly. Therefore, the more detailed and clear the proposal, the better the chances of securing the grant.

The purpose of writing this book was to create a ready guide on how to prepare a research proposal from the preparation stage to the final submission. This is the second in a series of short book guides that will help researchers with a specific topic, develop an effective research proposal, counsel and invite them to value-added webinars, and share additional resources.

Academic research consultancy services offer coaching to anyone interested in starting research. This includes advice on how to choose a research topic, review literature, write a proposal, write the thesis, and prepare for the viva voce examination. The team of experts can guide you through the step-by-step process. We provide short sessions on 'how to' of all the activities related to dissertation and thesis writing. Undergraduate students may avail themselves of the services of their projects. If you have any queries, you can book a free one-on-one meeting at sumanmundkur.com and get your answers. Researchers at any stage in their research journey can seek help.

TABLE OF CONTENTS

Chapter 1: INTRODUCTION

“If I have seen further than others, it is by standing upon the shoulders of giants."

- Sir Isaac Newton (1675)

What Newton meant by the word “giant” is that the researchers who came before him contributed immensely to the scientific community. He acknowledged their contribution to knowledge. He relied on the ideas of other scientists who came before him to build his own. Being a genius, he knew that his scientific contributions were not from him alone. His curiosity and thirst for knowledge led him to his numerous scientific discoveries.

Sir Isaac Newton’s contribution to science was significant during his lifetime (1661-1727). He gave a deeper understanding of astronomy, chemistry, mathematics, physics and theology, calculus, optics, and the gravitational forces that scientists use today. It was not just theorizing the laws; he laid the groundwork for other scientists like Einstein to build upon these theories. Newton's three laws of motion have enabled the scientists after him to understand the movement of subatomic particles to spiralling galaxies! (1).

Research is about building upon the knowledge that exists.

Research in any field must take into account what other researchers have established in their respective fields. **The journey of every research scholar who wishes to take up doctoral studies, dissertations, or research projects must begin with preparing a proposal on a chosen topic for research.**

What is a proposal?

A proposal is a research plan specially drafted as a formal document that is put forward convincingly for consideration by others. The reader must know that you are a confident academic writer, thinker and know what is expected in your field of study to plan your academic life (2). The academic proposal will generally be communicated in a formal tone, written in the third person, with clarity and focus on the topic, with a clear choice of words to keep it concise, and drafted in a prescribed format along with citations (3).

Most commonly asked questions on Academic proposal writing

Some of the most frequently asked questions by scholars on research proposals are listed as follows. How do I write a proposal on a topic I am new to? How do I write a good proposal? Why is it necessary to submit a research proposal? When is it required? What is the primary purpose? Who will read it? How does one ensure the proposal is not rejected? What should I avoid while writing a proposal? How to write a successful research proposal? What should I include in a research proposal? How do I draft a proposal?

Apart from the commonly asked questions about the proposal, find tips on how to make it more effective and ensure it stands out and is approved. This book attempts to answer those questions, serves as a guide, and helps develop an effective research proposal. You will be guided through each of the components of the proposal. Once you have understood the process of preparing for the outline and structure, you will find the process simple.

Purpose of writing the proposal

The primary purpose is to communicate to the reader what the research is about. The objective of the research proposal is to convince the reader. The reader may be a supervisor or an expert in the academic field, a reviewer or from the funding agency.

There are different types of proposals. Particularly in business, there are formally solicited, informally solicited, and unsolicited proposals (5). Academic research proposals may be explorative, argumentative, analytical, narrative, or descriptive in the writing style. However, research proposals have to be persuasive (6). The style of preparing a proposal will change with the very purpose. The objective for which the proposal is being made.

A research proposal must have a detailed plan of how the research will be conducted. It has to be presented in a structured, clear, and concise manner.

Suppose you are at the stage of developing a topic for research. In that case, it is suggested that you first select a topic. You can read the first book in the series titled "**Zeroing in on a Research Topic**." It will help you with the skills needed, databases for literature search of resources, and strategies in selection. It will also help you narrow down the search and finalize a topic.

The research proposal must have an outline of your research plan. The outline will explain how you will research, the steps involved, the methods, procedures, equipment, etc. The duration of time required for each step, called a timeframe, will be displayed. Along with these, the proposal must describe how ethical guidelines will be followed during the research. It must be remembered that the proposal is not merely to seek approval and admission to a Ph.D. program, but a plan for Ph.D. research. Nevertheless, the outcome must be in the form of a thesis, dissertation or a research project.

Understanding the research process

When the researcher understands the clear purpose of the research, it becomes simpler to find ways of executing the research. Once you find a purpose for research, you will be motivated to write the rationale better. To achieve a successful research journey, motivation for the research is an essential ingredient for any researcher, regardless of the discipline.

In the proposal, you must explain why the research is needed. You will find the necessity for the research only after reading about the subject and finding what is missing, called the

research gap. You must continue reading on the topic until you have identified a clear gap in research. Then you need to show the following three aspects:

* How will your research add to knowledge by filling that **gap**/or gaps in research?
* What **additional value** will your research add to the existing knowledge?
* Is there **a solution** you seek to solve a problem that has been identified?
* If there is a solution, is there a better, cheaper, faster, **more efficient solution** that you are trying to find?

By reading about the subject, there will be a better understanding of the research topic. Through a **literature review**, you display your understanding of the subject. You show that you are going to learn much more during the research. The review must be more detailed and extensive in a Ph.D. proposal compared to the Master's dissertation.

* The proposal must have an **outline of your research methodology**. The outline will explain how you will do research, the steps involved, the method, the procedures, equipment, the

standards used for procedures and testing, the evaluation and analysis, etc. The duration of time required for each step, called a **timeframe**, will be displayed.

* The proposal must also explain how will **ethical issues** be addressed and provide an assurance that during the research, **no harm** to the people, animals, or the planet will be done.

* These are the **essential elements** that every proposal must include. Even before starting with research, all these aspects must be approved by the University Committee or the evaluating body, administrators, guides, or supervisors.

Research readiness

A research proposal is one of discovering the potential for research by the researcher. Therefore, it is all the more critical that it is **well-thought, well-planned, and well presented**. The preparation and development of the proposal itself calls for **self-study**, which is an essential component of Ph.D. research.

Often, in my experience as a research consultant, Ph.D. aspirants are in a rush to submit the research proposal. A good proposal can be made only after extensive reading and planning. Sufficient and focused time must be given to creating a winning proposal. Compressing and presenting concisely and clearly shows the researcher's preparedness.

Grant Andrews (2017) suggested to those researchers concerned about the task of thesis writing, can get a free report on your strengths and challenges. This will help be better prepared by being mindful of your challenges and capitalizing on your strengths. It will make you aware of the areas where you need to work on yourself before starting the thesis. Before you start your thesis writing, it may be a good idea to take a readiness survey (2).

A well-planned proposal

A proposal is a plan submitted by a researcher for approval from a concerned institution, university, funding body, or agency. The plan to be submitted must be detailed in every aspect so that the deciding authority or decision-makers are clear on the researcher's thought process. The proposal conveys how well-thought-out the plan is and, most importantly, whether it is achievable. The proposal will take its course in the next few months and up to three or four years of your academic life.

According to Grant Andrews (2017), since your academic life is going to be planned out of the proposal, it is essential to get it right the first time. All the parts must be included so that your supervisor and the administrators or review committee will approve (2).

The University Research and Recognition Committee, administrators and supervisors, or a team of subject experts, will give the approval. The proposal must prove to them that the research will significantly contribute. The certification will eventually be granted by the academic institution, which may have invested heavily in the research facilities like laboratories, equipment, and technical staff to handle it, as well as resources in the physical form of books, journals, and online resources through training and subscriptions.

Persuasion in proposal writing

Writing a persuasive proposal is critical in business promotion, just as proposal writing is required for business. Advertising, marketing, seeking, and offering contracts for goods and services is somewhat impossible without a proposal. In academic proposals, the same degree of persuasiveness helps convince the reviewers of the importance of the research and seek approval. Proposals are meant to convince the reader to approve them (3).

How to be persuasive in academic proposal writing?

An effective proposal involves formulating sound arguments around the topic of research. The language must be convincing; the need must be strongly stated; the purpose of the research must be clearly stated; an element of urgency in finding solutions to the identified problems. "Sure to make a difference," "effective use," "ready solution," and "trust the efficiency" are vital in persuading and convincing the reader.

The following chapter will look at the preparation required before writing a proposal. In research consulting, I have seen some aspiring to seek admission for a Ph.D. struggle with certain aspects of drafting the proposal and seek help only when the deadline is too close. This book will save you from the struggles.

You can easily develop the proposal after viewing a sample format and understanding the finer details. You should understand how to prepare for the different sections of the proposal so that you can draft it confidently and independently.

Summary

* **The research proposal demonstrates that you are now ready to start research by describing the plan of conducting each procedure with the timeframe for each research activity.**
* **The literature review must show a clear need for conducting the research and how the study will add to knowledge by bridging the research gaps.**
* **The proposal shows the researcher's understanding of the subject through the background information, identification, and statement of the problem.**
* **The proposal must explain how it will help solve a problem or add value to what is already known.**
* **The research proposal must be persuasive to convince the readers**

of the value and the research potential that the proposed work will carry. An academic research proposal must convince the reader.

* **Academic research work submitted as a thesis, dissertation, or project will bear the name of the institutions and universities granting the qualification.**

* **Educational institutions make significant investments in research infrastructure and resources. The research proposal must show that the resources will be utilized.**

* **If seeking financial assistance or grants, it should show that it is worth investing in your research.**

* **Better research preparedness will help you write the research proposal more smoothly without being constrained or feeling trapped.**

Chapter 2: PREREQUISITES FOR A PROPOSAL FOR RESEARCH

Better preparedness will make it easier for the researcher to write more effectively. So let us understand why some proposals get approved for admission into a doctoral program, how only a few projects get approved, and how only a few selected proposals secure funding. What are the tricks that make them 'click'? This chapter lists what you need to keep ready before starting with writing down the proposal and maki ng it more effective.

A good proposal should be:

* Specific to solving a problem or filling up a research gap,
* Clear, concise, and free from any ambiguity,
* Crisp and to the point, adhere to the word count specified,
* Convincing in tone,
* Attainable considering the time given,
* Convey a vital element of self-study and exploration that is key to academic research,
* All sources of information have been acknowledged,

* Bring out an element of newness and innovation, and
* Persuade the reader to accept.

Being better prepared with the prerequisites will make the proposal smoother, faster, and more effective.

Motivation

The primary prerequisite is research motivation. Gear up your motivation and energy to do what will matter most shortly. The research will involve complete uninterrupted attention that will occupy most of your time. The motivation must be sustained, therefore, selecting and researching a topic that interests them most is best and setting goals.

If there is a chance to reset your priorities in life, now is the time for that makeover and shift in focus and lifestyle to that of a researcher.

Research Goals

Have clear **research goals**. Prepare to set a clearer vision of research by shifting your research focus–your goal post. Informative, inspirational, and directional, they are seeking to capitalize on the power of purpose. That power will drive a researcher to achieve the targeted outcomes. Why am I writing a proposal? Why do I want to research? What is it that you want to achieve? "Why" can be made stronger with affirmations that are read, heard, or repeated daily. The purpose of the proposal must be clear before starting to write.

Time and concentration

More critical will be managing time. Time and concentration will be critical in the next few years or months to come. Since it is **your time** and nobody can manage it better than you. Time allocation for small research activities like searching online within different related keywords, reading and reviewing, summary writing, organizing the resources, preparing a mind map, preparing the reference list, and downloading references will help. Setting aside a specific time and location to work is beneficial for increasing productivity. As a researcher, you will set standards for elevating yourself from being a student to a researcher, and from a researcher to a more productive researcher!

Research prior to research

Starting the proposal writing must be done only after researching secondary sources of information to build the subject's credibility.

Collecting data in graphs, charts, figures, and facts on the topic as backup support. This can help in proving that there is a problem to which you have a solution to propose. Since it is too early to state your views and suggestions, you will need the support of work that has already been done on the topic to convince the intended audience. Sometimes, you may need to gather data by conducting a pilot study or a survey to prove your point of view (7).

Academic writing for a proposal

Academic writing is not like any other type of essay. With the use of social media, texting, informal slang, and short forms have become acceptable among students. As researchers, it is important to become familiar with academic writing skills. The tips are to prepare the proposal rigorously, format it religiously, and proofread it ruthlessly (8). The important characteristics of academic writing and the dos and don'ts are well defined (3).

A research proposal for a Ph.D. requires the same effort, time, and input as writing a business proposal. The academic research proposal is similar and requires the same level of persuasion to be approved. Before starting to write the proposal, the guidelines provided by the University or Institution must be thoroughly understood. Even a minor deviation may result in the proposal not being accepted.

Universities, Institutions, and Research Organizations

After a survey of universities offering a Ph.D. program in your subject domain, you can shortlist. Each university's website will have to be checked for instructions on how to apply for admission, the procedure, the format, guidelines, etc. Instructions must be read carefully so that the applicant does not miss out on any. The application can be rejected based on non-compliance with the guidelines. If there is none, then a general format can be used so long as the relevant information is presented clearly. Clarity does matter!

Guidelines for Proposal Writing

Each university or educational institution has its own guidelines for proposal writing.

Each country and each university will have different ways of communicating. However, any proposal may have a few common points, regardless of the institute or country. The research proposal must convince the academic institutional authorities that the following three points are common:

1 Clarity on the proposed study: A clearly defined title must be framed even if it is tentative. What will be the focus of the research? What are the research questions to be addressed? The clarity in the method of gathering data, on what will be covered and what not.

2 Purpose of research on the selected topic: The purpose of research on the selected topic must be specified. Also, how to justify, as a lot has been done on this topic but not applied in this region, country, or industry. If the context has changed over the years, the time has changed. We need to revisit and verify the methodology, lacking in approach, sampling, or other methodological representation. Is it original, or are you replicating research done earlier? Solving a problem? Are you filling a gap?

3 The rationale for conducting the research is to fill a gap identified in the literature survey. Is there a novelty, originality and something new? Is the subject important and worth researching? Is it worthwhile to research? Is it going to add value to the existing body of knowledge? Is it manageable, achievable, and feasible within the resources? Why is it important?

Why has it not been done before? Is it unique?

Guidelines

Read the guidelines once again to understand before you are ready to start writing the proposal. If you still feel unsure, you can consult for tips on improving your skills and academic proposal writing.

Format

The prescribed format for preparing the proposal is more straightforward than preparing one without guidelines. The format may be available online. Submission of the proposal may be online or offline, often with a word limit to adhere to, for each component in the proposal. The formatting of the document must be consistent throughout the proposal.

Resources for the Review of Literature

However, much as we would like to, we cannot read and know all literature on the topic. Nevertheless, we can try to explore as many secondary resources as possible. During my research therefore, my supervisor encouraged me to discuss the research topic with as many experts as possible to be able to crystal down ideas. Several experts gave different perspectives during the personal discussions. Most had given a clear 'go-ahead with the topic' and provided mindful suggestions. Views from experts can be reassuring and encouraging!

Joel Chan, an Assistant Professor at the University of Maryland, College Park, suggested that one can turn to colleagues and other intelligent and motivated folks you admire and trust both in and outside your field. Discussion with them helps refine ideas and kill the ones that need to be killed (9).

A personalized academic library can be created with tools like Mendeley, Zotero, EndNote, R Discovery, and many others. The earlier three are referencing and citation tools. With R Discovery, by keying in the subject of interest, the top three related papers will be made available daily. You can download it on your mobile phone so you can catch up with reading even when traveling. The advantage is that while using the app on other devices, smooth web-app integration, bookmarking papers, and using smart summaries can be helpful for researchers to find resources (10). You can download R Discovery for free or use the web version at the link: https://app.adjust.net.in/3eju3so. Other useful products from Researcher.Life are listed in the Additional Resources section at the end.

Databases from Google Scholar, PubMed, Web of Science, SciFinder Scholar, UpToDate, PsycINFO, and Ovid MEDLINE, National Centre for Biotechnology Information (NCBI), Highwire Press archive (10), and more can be explored. In the first book in this series, titled 'Zeroing In On A Research Topic' has a Chapter devoted to listing down databases that are useful for research in any field of study.

You have now been introduced to the preparations you must make before writing the research proposal. You can imagine how much more productive and faster you as a researcher can be by making your preparedness before starting writing a proposal.

Seeking admission for a Ph.D. from abroad

If the plan is to apply to study abroad, you may want to consider the following points:

* Availability of the subject of specialization
* Ranking and Reputation of the University
* Experts and Supervisors at the relevant Department
* Infrastructure facilities

* Accommodation for international students
* Climatic conditions
* Availability of fee structure and funding assistance.

Elena Golovushkina's tips on writing a successful proposal, starts with listing the different Ph.D. programs abroad on PhDPortal.com. The comprehensive list gives over 9714 Ph.D. programs globally to explore (12). The discipline, title of the course, location of the university, the mode of instruction, online, on campus, or hybrid, the fees, duration, part-time or full-time format, and other details. Based on the criteria listed above, a handful can be short-listed with a priority. The proposal can be made based on the guidelines of the one topmost on the list.

A proposal, once made, must not be considered final. The basic structure remains the same, but the contents may be refined and revised several times before submitting to the University. Securing admission to Ph.D. does not mean that the proposal is final. Before starting the Ph.D. work the expert research panel must approve the proposal. Researchers must be prepared to be flexible enough to make drastic changes based on the inputs from the expert panel arranged by the university. Revising the proposal will certainly bring more clarity and define goals.

Research for a topic selection can give several ideas that would not have come otherwise. Primary sources of data from scholarly literature could be best to begin with. Libraries and the Internet are the places to look for content. The library of your institution can be a great source of resources. I recommend you become friends with the librarian. You need to have identified a broad research area of your interest. Being a regular at the college library and being friends with the librarian opened up a lot of resources for me. On several occasions, he would keep some reference articles like magazine articles and research papers ready for my next visit. I had some pdf files related to my topic sent to me by email. A professor who is knowledgeable and willing to give time to discuss the scope of research and trending research areas will help. A professional research consultant will guide you through the drafting of the proposal until submission (13).

A lot will depend on how you can identify and respond to the gaps in knowledge through your research based on the background. The summarization of literature reviews can be a strong basis to support the aim of the proposed research.

In Chapter 3, you will see how to structure the different components of the research proposal. Each component of the proposal has been detailed. See how you can make it more effective and achieve success.

You will be explained how to draft your methodology, methods of gathering data, sample, analyze, and prepare a time frame. You will also learn how to formulate your reference list immediately. If you work with this complete guide, you will be able to write an effective research proposal.

Prepare your own 'to-do checklist' as you prepare to write the proposal.

Summary

* **Success is assured when the motivation for research, a clear goal, focus, and time are clearly defined.**

* **Shortlist Universities where you will apply for research. Check the website for Subjects, Courses, Faculty, and their research experience, ranking, and reputation.**

* **Look for the prescribed format on the Institution's or university**

website. Understanding and adhering to the

* **guidelines laid out while writing the proposal is essential.**

* **For a successful proposal, preparations will be necessary, as will adequate time plan.**

* **Time and concentration are two critical ingredients to success in the research process.**

* **Clarity, purpose, and rationale are the features common to research proposals.**

* **Preparation in creating your personalized library by exploring databases for content online will be most beneficial.**

* **More time will be needed to explore options if the plan is to study abroad. Before beginning to write, research and shortlist universities' websites, download their guidelines, and become acquainted with them.**

Chapter 3: COMPONENTS AND STRUCTURE OF A RESEARCH PROPOSAL

A research proposal is made up of different segments or components. Each component of the proposal is vital for developing a research proposal. In this chapter, we see each of the components in detail. This will help understand the components that build the proposal structure. The information needed for the research proposal is more or less the same, regardless of whether the proposal is for an application for an academic program like M.Phil., M.S, or Ph.D., or a research project funding.

The components of the research proposal are listed below:

Title Page

The title page should contain the name of the scholar and the level the proposal is being submitted for. It must have the name of the university or institution and the department to which it is submitted. Some proposals also include the logo, which is unnecessary unless it is in the format provided. The date of submission can be mentioned at the end of the page alternatively the academic year. It can also include the recipient of the proposal and contact information. The name of the Supervisor or Guide in case they have already been assigned.

Title

The title must be catchy and attract the reader. The title conveys precisely what the research is about. The limit should not exceed 15 words unless specified in the university guidelines. A fairly rough title can be given for the intended research, which can be revised later. Ideally, the title should be given at the end, after the research proposal is ready for submission, so it is worded precisely. The title should not be so broad that the reader does not understand the scope of the study. At the same time, it should not be too short to limit its scope. Revising the title during the research even after acceptance and admission to the course is possible. This may involve a procedure submitted through the supervisor or guide.

Abstract

The abstract and the title together can impact the reader. If the title draws the readers' attention, they will go on to read the abstract. So, the Abstract is the face of the research proposed. An abstract may be 100-300 words and includes a couple of sentences to introduce the subject and a clear statement of the need or purpose for conducting the research. It can be a problem statement or a question/s that need to be addressed. A broad methodology of how the research will be conducted and, finally, the expected findings of the research.

Keywords

The keywords may be limited to five and arranged in alphabetical order. The words can be synonyms or terms related to the research title. Researchers often tend to repeat the words in the title or the abstract, which is unnecessary. The keywords help in the searchability of your research by other researchers. Keywords must be carefully selected if you want your thesis to be cited later.

Introduction to the Topic of Research

The first thing that the introduction should do is hook the reader and capture their interest. The introduction should briefly describe what the research is about. It could begin with what? Questions like: What is this study going to be about? What is the area of research? What are the different ideas that other researchers have addressed and are still working on? There are different ways of introducing the research topic. Depending on the nature of the subject, the following point strategies may be used:

  * The historical and current situation will provide a clear backdrop for the proposal's evaluators.
  * The introduction can also begin with a global overview of the research on the topic and the local perspective.

* The introduction can start with interesting facts that will make the reader think about the topic.
* The introduction can begin with a list of issues and concerns affecting daily lives that you find significant and warrant further investigation. What is the main point that you want to bring forth?
* How will the research attempt to fill a gap in the literature?
* The identified problem, as well as the urgency of finding a solution, must be studied. Why the problem is being addressed needs to be resolved through research.
* What is the current state in the body of knowledge, or has it already been researched? Can you include the topic's novelty, trend, or status?

* The research questions that can be answered.

The **introduction can start broad and end narrow**, with the need for research. Stating the need gives the research proposal a direction. This is where you express your area of interest in the research topic or subject.

The introduction to the research must be presented in such a way that the scholar seems excited about the proposed research. The researcher can express what is exciting about the research topic or what has motivated the researcher to select the topic for research. What was your motivation for researching this topic? The reason for conducting this research and the direction in which you would like to take it.

The background of the research and context

The background and context may or may not be expected in all research proposals. However, this component gives a brief overview of the general study area within which the proposed study is included. The background outline must be in the academic context of the proposed research. Specific terms, operational definitions, and concepts can be defined at this stage to make it easy for the reader to understand.

The researcher must critically review the empirical literature on the historical data available. A researcher must display an understanding of the theoretical literature that has been studied. Resources may be from the thesis, dissertations, or research papers published in reputed journals. This must be done carefully; one cannot be casual while reading. At a later stage, this reading will help design the present study while appearing for the interview for the admission process.

Alternatively, if the historical background is not expected, you can include 'What is known in this area?' Here you can give the present state of knowledge. It allows for the summarization of some recent research and provides critical comments on what was missing and the gaps identified by the proposed research.

You can add some debate about the latest research in this area. This component can show the researcher's understanding and familiarity with the subject, clarity of thought, and expression while communicating the ideas. The reader gets a chance to read the depth of information collected by the researcher.

The need to solve the problem has been mentioned in the introduction section. However, in this section, a precise description, and understanding of how important this research will be in solving the problem and addressing other issues will be provided.

How will it be essential to explain and understand the problem? To what extent is the problem going to be solved? What is the contribution of the proposed research? Why is this research necessary? What will the research address? How will this research help? Is it also possible to state how this research will be unique? Which part of the research will address what other researchers have not done, studied, or not found? The background will show that it is worthwhile conducting this research.

Literature Review

The goal of the literature review is to provide a critical discussion and researcher perspective, not just to identify who did what. There should be extensive research reviews by prominent scholars in the field in recent years. All the details may not be given, but the key findings from each research study may be summarized.

The review of relevant literature can be a part of the background section, a separate section, or as recommended in the guidelines. If no guidelines are prescribed, the two, historical background and review, can be merged under the side-heading 'Background'. The sequence of developments can be presented in chronological order. The review must not be very general and broad. It will seem vague to the reader. The review must be specific and cover all the important ideas around the chosen topic under research.

The three essential functions of a literature review are:

* Provide a background and basis for research.
* Research questions should emerge from the review of literature.
* Objectives of the proposed research.

A research question can be in the form of a hypothesis or exploratory in nature. This will be statistically tested, proved, and accepted or rejected.

Problem Statement

Write the problem statement in a concise form. It must be clearly stated. In the statement, it is better to avoid adjectives and adverbs (12). Reviewers want to know the background and the **specific problem** that needs to be addressed. What matters is how significant it is or what impact it will have. The statement that conveys the **objective** of the study. How do you intend to solve the problem, and what is your approach to finding solutions? The conclusive remarks can be on how the topic itself can contribute to solving key issues.

Objectives

* Objectives must be specific rather than general and vague.

 Objectives must be SMART: Specific, Measurable, Attainable / Achievable, Reliable, and Time-bound.

* The main objectives can also be broken down into logically arranged sub-objectives.
* Describe the objectives in terms of those that suggest change, modification, improvement, transformation, action, and so on.

* Objectives could be revolutionary or could be to provide recommendations.

Research Questions

The main aim and related research questions should guide the research proposal flow. A review of literature helps the researcher identify the research questions. During self-study, by reading prior research work, the researcher may come across a question in mind that is not answered. There may be some problems that need solutions. If solutions are provided, it is unclear whether they will work in another similar context. One may find that these are gaps that the proposed research can fill.

Jotting down questions that come to mind is a good habit. The list of questions can then be organized according to their importance, with one central theme and related or supporting questions. There can also be sub-questions. If there are many research questions, they can be grouped based on sub-themes.

There is no limit to the number of questions. This is a crucial stage in research as it guides the course of the subsequent actions. The approach that the researcher will follow will be guided.

Before starting to write the problem statement, it is better to reflect on these fundamental questions, as they will guide the course of proposal writing. The questions must be specific, providing a central theme and related questions. The research questions will also guide the formulation of the problem statement, the hypothesis, and the approach to answering those questions through research. Narrow down and see if the study is feasible at the given time and available resources.

Problem Statement

The problem statement outlines and addresses what the problem is about. The goal is to define a specific problem that can be solved through focused research and careful decision-making which is well explained in the Editage Insights podcast titled 'How to write a statement of problem for your research proposal' (10). Writing a problem statement is well explained in another article by Henry Bwisa on the Editage Insights podcast titled 'How to write a statement of problem for your research proposal'. The statement of the problem may be in three parts. The first part will state the ideal situation and how things should be. The second part describes the present state of affairs or the present situation that needs to be addressed. The third part identifies how the researcher intends to improve upon an ideal situation (11). Regardless of the subject discipline, once the topic under research and the problem is identified, this resource can be explored and applied effectively.

Hypothesis

The statement of your hypothesis can be done to either support or challenge your research findings. Formulation of the hypothesis must be done carefully in consultation with an expert. Every research proposal need not have a hypothesis. There can be more than one hypothesis to be tested, depending on the subject of research.

Research Methods

Research methods are part of the overall research design. **Research design is an outline of the research proposed.** The methods used in collecting data according to the objectives. For example, in an exploratory study on consumer awareness, the survey method will be suitable. Nevertheless, when you have to study consumer buying practices, interview methods will help in capturing better insights.

The **methodological tools and techniques** used by other researchers may be cited here. In which case, the **questionnaire and interview schedule** will be the tools for **collecting research data**. The use of appropriate tools will help in achieving the objective. You will then justify why the tool was developed, selected, or found appropriate compared to other tools for data collection followed by the basis for the selection of a sampling strategy and the sample size. Again, the context will aid in identifying **the sources of information, and textual and visual data** are drawn from both primary and secondary sources. **The standard or standard operating procedures** followed universally may be guiding the methods.

You may encounter likely problems while collecting data, and how you would overcome them is to say, if Plan A does not work, then Plan B. Likely problems you foresee while conducting experimental trials or gathering field data while conducting research must be mentioned here.

Early researchers find this part of the research proposal writing challenging. A Researcher.Life Blog by Aditya Joshi titled 'What is Research Methodology: Learn How to Choose Research Methods provides examples on choosing the right methodology, provided the problem statement or hypothesis is clear and well defined. Just to understand how to choose the right methodology for your research problem, to help you on 'How to Choose the Best

Research Methodology for your study, understand better and select' (14).

Research Design

The research design is like a blueprint of the method and sequence in which the proposed research will be conducted. This is one of the most critical components of the research proposal. The researchers are expected to submit original work. The choice of a research design depends on the field of study chosen.

Methodology

It should outline the broad methodology used, be it **qualitative, quantitative, or a mixed methodology**, that will guide the course of the research work.

Research methods

The data will be sourced from both **primary and secondary sources**. It will be explained in greater detail how and what the procedure for conducting research will be. The sequence of steps in the procedure must go in parallel to the objectives that have been logically listed. When there is a word limit, the information can be in the form of a flowchart.

This section includes all the methodological **tools and techniques** that will be used to meet each of the study's objectives. A justification of why these tools or techniques were selected is necessary. It is not difficult to identify the methods or tools used by other researchers in the field before selecting the most appropriate for the proposed study.

The research design will specify whether it will be **library-based, field-based, or laboratory-based experimental research** and will explain the materials and method in which the research will be conducted.

On library-based research, the University of Birmingham, UK, shares on their website a few examples. Library-based research methods will include visiting particular libraries or archives, fieldwork, or interviews. The library-based research proposal should explain where the essentialresources (e.g., case study reports, journal articles) are located (in the School of Social Work Library) (13).

In any laboratory-based experimental research, the **materials and methods** used will be specified. The **standard experimental procedures and evaluation methods** must be elaborated. The idea is that any other researcher must be able to replicate the study and get the same findings. Therefore, there is a lot of emphasis on validity and reliability in research.

Suppose the plan is to conduct fieldwork or collect **empirical data**. In that case, details should be provided (e.g., if you plan to **conduct interviews in a survey**, who will you interview? How many interviews will you conduct? Will there be access problems?). The approach, direction, and focus of research will change accordingly.

Sampling design

This will specify the population, and the samples will be selected. The sampling strategy is used to select a representative sample of the population. This part also covers the likely problems you may face in sample selection and how you could overcome them. Methods in which the samples will be approached and data gathered.

Analysis design

You should explain how you are going to analyze your research findings. Some issues may have to be dealt with subjectively, while others must be dealt with objectively. How will the statistical analysis be carried out, as well as the types of statistics that will be used in the study?

Time frame

A clear plan of all the research activities from the beginning of the initial to the submission of the thesis should be reflected in the timeline. Specifically, time line starts from the initiation of topic approval and registration to the submission of the project/thesis or dissertation. The time frame plan is essential and shows that the objectives are met within the timeline. Research, otherwise, can never end and go on and on. If the time frame is presented as a paragraph or table, it will be specified in the guidelines. In either the paragraph or table form, it should contain the stages.

Chapter Outline

The sequence of each chapter in the thesis, as they will appear in the thesis and a brief outline of what each of them will contain can be listed. The chapters communicate the contents and flow of research. The reviewer will know exactly how the content will be organized.

Limitations of the study

The limitations of the study must be listed down. It is impossible to claim that any one research study is complete. There is always a scope for further study. Any research study is intended to add to the body of knowledge. Research is valuable. The scope and limitations set the boundaries, and the readers know what to expect from the study.

Significance of the study

In my experience, I have seen some proposals with this section following the statement of the problem. The proposal must show why the research study is essential. It must answer: to whom will this matter and how? Who will benefit from this research? How will the findings affect you? What is the difference it will make to the existing knowledge? What will it add to what is known? What is the expected outcome? What will be the impact? How will it impact you?

In Social Science, for example, will it affect society? If so, which section of society-the children, the women, the distressed, the under-privileged, the minority, the ill, the affected, the distressed, the poor or the deprived?

For example, a study pertaining to water pollution in the area of environmental science, would involve research in to finding solutions to the following questions: What is the problem? Who is affected? In what way is it affecting? How was the effect noticed? What were the reactions? What are the possible solutions? Which solutions were tried and did not work or partially solved? Why is it important to find a better solution? How is it going to impact?

The *significance in terms of the originality* of the proposed research is primary to the *novelty of the research* proposed. Therefore, explaining how your ideas were built upon and will add to the present knowledge is vital. Another tip to go in here will be the need to show how and why it is *timely* to research with an *element of urgency*.

Summary and Conclusion

A summary of the research includes the significance of the study identified, brief background, problem identified, how this research proposes to address the problem, methodology and methods to gather data. **The research's expected outcome is the change and contribution to the social,**

economic, cultural, educational, or environmental spheres.

Bibliography

At the end of the proposal, a short list of references that have been referred to, and only those mentioned in the background component of the proposal should be listed down. You may list down journal articles, books, magazines, and other online resources from websites separately.

The bibliographical references must be formatted well in the **referencing style** recommended in the guidelines. Each reference must start with the name of the first alphabet of the author's surname. The style should be consistent in using punctuation, italics, and sequence. Formatting errors can stand out even if the rest of the proposal is formatted well.

A word limit in the reference section of a proposal can be limited to only the work **cited in the proposal**. A lot of prior research work may be relevant but may be excluded from referencing. Only the most relevant resources that have been cited need to be included here. The focus will be on fine-tuning the quality of research references rather than the numbers or quantity.

The challenge will include a blend of theoretical, empirical, and methodological work that is relevant to your research proposal.

If there is no limitation to the number of pages in the research proposal, all the relevant literature you referred to and may want to refer to for your thesis may be included. The reference may then be about two pages for a master's dissertation and more pages for a Ph.D. thesis proposal. However, the references for the final submission of the dissertation and thesis may be much more.

Proof-reading

Proof-reading is a very important aspect of any document submitted for approval, especially the research proposal. Often, aspiring research scholars work on the proposal content till the date of submission, leaving limited time for this important activity. This is important because a proposal with errors can be the reason for rejection. There are several online tools that are available to get this checked for grammar, punctuation, long or ambiguous statements.

Plagiarism free

The proposal must be free from plagiarism. The researcher may have to sign an undertaking in this regard. It is better to be aware from the start. The undertaking is a self-certification that the research proposal is his or her own work. An undertaking that the proposal is liable to be screened for plagiarism if any unfair means have been used, and it will result in application rejection.

The declaration may read as:

> *"I hereby declare that the research proposal submitted to the Department of.............................., Institute...................., is my own work, written in my own words. The proposal is based on my self-study on the research topic. I have given due credit to all the contributors of literature and the materials used in the preparation of the proposal.*
>
> *I understand that my research proposal may be screened for plagiarism and other unfair practices, which can result in the cancellation of my application to the course of......................."*

The proposal's clarity presents a lot of the preparedness for research. It conveys the readiness on the part of the researcher to conduct research. A well-thought-out proposal is more likely to be approved. Suppose you have drafted the proposal, including the above components in the expected format, and are still unsure. In that case, you can **schedule a complimentary session** at sumanmundkur.com and send in a preliminary **review request.** You can seek counselling, guidance, and suggestions on improving your research writing for any assistance in your research journey.

Online submission

When the format is available online, it is better to prepare the responses on a word file and copy each response into the online form. This enables you to make revisions and improvements at any stage till the submission button is hit. The content can be copied and pasted on the online research proposal form provided at the time of submission.

Most often, online or offline forms have a word count limit. The responses must adhere to the **word limit**, particularly if the proposal has to be submitted online. Any extra word will not be allowed in an online submission.

Developing the responses on a word file allows for review and modification before they are uploaded and submitted. It will allow the applicant to save a draft copy of the submitted proposal for future reference, or the information will be lost.

Online submissions can be made only once; therefore, making them error-proof without any spelling or grammatical errors is important. Errors can convey to the decision makers that the candidate is not very particular about such an important document. This is a summary, or a gist, of what must be included. A word file is always useful for saving a draft of what has been submitted for future reference.

Grant proposal

While writing a proposal for grants, it is better to shortlist where you would like to apply for funding by going through the websites of funding bodies. Special attention must be paid to the objectives of the funding agency. Check the website to see whether the research you propose fits into the funding objectives.

A grant proposal will need additional inputs from the components described above. Grant proposals need a detailed budget plan that needs to be communicated. With all the budget heads, one-time and recurring expenses under each head will have to be specified. This book is specific to academic proposal writing for a Ph.D. or a post-graduate research project.

Money is not the only thing. A lot of time and effort goes into preparing a proposal for research or funding! Preparing the proposal also teaches you many other skills for better preparedness for conducting extensive research. Writing a research proposal helps you prepare for a comprehensive examination or personal interview that the researcher will have to face before registering for the post-graduate program or Ph.D. program. In the next chapter you will find some checklists and tips on how to make your proposal draft.

Summary

* **Each of the components in the structure of a research proposal is important. Each component is linked to each other to bring a flow to the proposal document.**

* **A brief introduction to your topic is sufficient for any layperson unfamiliar with the subject. The**

introduction may be given as a historical background or the chronological order of development. The introduction gives the context and a general overview of the topic.

* The background of the study summarizes your reading of the literature on prior research and understanding of the topic. It illustrates the research done by previous researchers in the field, based on which you propose to build your research.

* The review must be specific and cover all of the important ideas around the chosen research topic.

* The problem statement must clearly show the gaps in research or the problem that your research seeks to resolve.

* The Objectives must be specific, measurable, achievable, reliable, and time-bound. They must be defined clearly, with the main and sub-objectives, if any.

* Objectives that suggest any kind of change, modification, improvement, transformation, action, or recommendations are appealing.

* Hypothesis statements can be listed. Statistical analysis must be proven in support or challenged by the research results.

* The research design is a plan of the procedure and sequence in which the proposed research will be conducted and comprises of the sources of data, methodology, research methods, data collection tools, sampling techniques, and so on.

* Validity of results and reliability in research must be ensured.

* The study's limitations and scope are to communicate the boundaries of your research.

* Chapter numbers and content must be in a logical sequence with a brief outline of each chapter.

* **Plan a realistic, and manageable timeframe as you will be required to submit the progress of research work on regular basis.**

* **The conclusion can be a brief of the proposed study, from the introduction to the expected outcome of research.**

* **The reference list must be in alphabetical order and formatted according to guidelines.**

* **Consider using supporting information such as developed research tools, certifications, pilot study reports, etc., as annexures to the proposal.**

* **Once the draft research proposal is ready, you will be able to present it convincingly and be ready to start your research journey by putting the plan into action.**

Chapter 4: TIPS TO MAKE YOUR PROPOSAL REJECTION FREE

Hundreds of applications are received by universities and research institutions each year. A team of experts in the subject are specifically assigned the task of selecting a few, depending on the intake capacity. The few get selected on the basis of certain criteria, which may not be known to researchers. However, the research proposal can be drafted to the best of one's ability. This chapter has some checklists that will help develop a winning proposal.

The research proposal

The research proposal may be submitted online or as a hard copy. In either case, the **title page** is the first thing that the reviewers are going to see. The **title** must be catchy and the layout of the title page visually appealing. The font size and style, along with the general impression, make the first impression. The organisation of the **content page**, the introduction and the other **components of the proposal** must be **engaging** enough to hold the reviewers' attention. The text in each component can be separated by paragraphs. **Side-headings in bold** make the text look organised. To make it **interesting, graphs and images** can be added with the source, figure number, and title.

Sufficient **white space** around the visuals and text paragraphs adds to the **visual appeal** of the proposal document. While listing down tools, methods, or materials, numbering them in sequence or use of bullet points looks better organised. Remember that the proposal must stand apart from several other proposals (4).

Presentation of the proposal

The research proposal may be presented in the form of a word document, in the format of an oral presentation, or both. An oral presentation to a panel of experts or a research committee requires preparation in terms of presenting a power-point presentation which will have the slides in the same format as the proposal in word format. The presentation can be made concise in the area of the review of the literature. Just like the manuscript, the slide presentation must have the following titles. A checklist for the sequence of slides:

* Title slide
* Introduction
* Need and significance of the study
* Rationale
* Review of Literature
* Research Questions
* Objectives
* Methodology

* Resources/ Infrastructure/ Collaboration sought
* Method of data collection and sampling
* Analysis design
* Expected results
* Time frame
* Conclusion
* Acknowledgment
* References
* Annexures, if any.

What reviewers will look for in the proposal?

A researcher must understand what is in the reviewer's mind and what they are looking for in the proposal. The reviewer or anybody reading your proposal must get:

* The first impression of the research proposal must be good.
* Clear your thoughts and communicate with the researcher.
* Be knowledgeable about your subject and understand what to expect from your research.
* It would be best if you sounded confident as an independent thinker, researcher, and writer.
* Clearly stated objectives, as well as a research design describing how they will be met
* Outlining the study's limitations and scope, thereby establishing clear research boundaries.
* Specifying the resources (library, equipment, and infrastructure) that will be purchased, hired, or collaborated on.

* Finally, state the impact of the research. If it helped solve multiple problems or impacted other disciplines it would make it a multi-disciplinary study.
* The potential for additional research and the prospects for field research.
* Plagiarism detection report.

The basis for rejection of a research proposal

* The title is too broad or does not specify the scope.
* The abstract lacks clarity and depth in its content (15).
* A topic introduction that fails to pique the reader's interest, as well as a presentation that fails to keep the audience's attention. A lengthy introduction that fails to capture.
* Relevance of the Topic.
* Vague subject area, scope and limitations of the study.
* The scope of the study may not have clarity.
* The language is inadequate. The proposal is not clear.
* Lacks in-text citations, inconsistent style, or improper citations and references.

* Failure to adhere to guidelines.
* Another grey area could be the methodology and the clarity in actions that will be taken during research.
* The language used may not be academic with a formal tone. Usage of short forms and slang.
* The formation and wording of sentences reveal a lot about a person's command of the language and ability to communicate.
* General organization of the proposed layout and presentation of the document.
* The outcome or impact of the research is unclear if the proposal does not indicate the critical contributions that the research could make.
* Proofreading and polishing. A proposal drafted in a rush to submit reflects last minute work.
* Formatting, page layout, margins, consistent space between paragraphs, images and textual content, and title of tables and the table.

It is better to get the draft proofread and edited by one of the family members and friends, and then again by an expert on the subject before submission. I have suggested to my clients that they get it read by anyone with a good command of the English language and who is willing to read, mark for corrections, and suggest improvements, even if they are from a different subject domain.

A reviewer expected some statistical basis and rejected particular group proposals with a 'hoped-for result in mind.' Unless the reviewers see value in the anticipated outcome, they will not likely accept the proposal (13).

Always have your plan B as a backup. As recommended in Chapter 1, shortlist at least three universities that offer the subject of your interest and specialization. You should be able to apply to another university.

Researchers may put in hard, thoughtful work and spend a lot of time proposing. The proposal being rejected can be disheartening. Being prepared to face rejection and improve on the proposal can be a blessing in disguise. It gives a further opportunity to overcome any missing link, fill the gaps, or fix the problem that may not have been foreseen. Feedback from reviewers must be taken positively (15).

In the case of grant proposals, the same tips apply. Funding agencies are interested in the impact the research will have on society. Collaborative and multi-disciplinary research proposals are better considered.

Editage Insights provides resources to help researchers understand how to avoid the rejection of grant proposals. The article also provides the features of a grant proposal and tips on the next steps in case the proposal is rejected (16). You can get some top tips on how to avoid grant proposal rejection that are applicable to proposals for Ph.D. research proposal (17).

Resume

Some proposals may require the researcher to provide a brief resume along with the research proposal. However, suppose the university or institute does not expect that. In that case, it is possible to add in the research design how your personal experiences, social environment, and personality have helped shape and led to the entire blueprint of research and how this will help in research with a subjective and objective approach to the topic. Communication with your passion for research will be appreciated.

Samples of Research Proposals

Although these samples of research proposals give an idea of what a proposal looks like, you will see a vast variation. Proposals are expected in different formats and lengths by different institutions. It is advisable to download the guidelines and follow them while developing your unique style.

Summary

Tips for developing an effective research proposal for a Ph.D. will help you with what to do and how.

Some of the best practises can be applied to any research proposal, whether to an academic institution or a funding agency.

As a researcher, you can maximize the tips listed in this chapter. Knowing what the reviewers expect helps shape the proposal so that the chances of possible rejection are minimized.

Most grants from funding agencies have strict criteria that must be understood before applying.

Researchers can use the checklist for the presentation sequence of slides in case you are shortlisted for Ph.D. admission or the research grant.

Some links to samples of research proposals provided will give some ideas. But developing an effective research proposal in your style can make it stand out!

CONCLUSION

An academic proposal shows why the research is needed and how it will be carried out. The important components of introduction convey what is the subject about, what is yet to be researched and the purpose of the research. The review of published literature describes what is already known in that chosen field. The Methodology, research design and the time and budget plan demonstrate how prepared the researcher is to start research.

Preparing a proposal is an excellent learning experience; many skills are developed through proposal writing. It can be daunting, starting from conceiving an idea to the topic selection and going through the proposal writing stages. However, first-time researchers require some guidance in the finer details while preparing the proposal.

Ready formats will be available on the university website. Specific guidelines may be provided. Whether the proposal is written to a university, research institute, the guidelines recommended must be adhered to strictly.

In developing the best proposal, you can see some examples of proposals from others. However, getting a proposal close to your subject area *may be problematic*. ***The best is***

to be original and unique in writing your research proposal.

This book must be used as a preparatory guide (Chapter 2) to the components and format of the research proposal (Chapter 3) and as a source of helpful tips for drafting an effective proposal (Chapter 4) and making it rejection-free.

Proposal writing must begin with a thorough understanding of the finer details of drafting. The tone must be formal but the language persuasive, as the chief purpose is to convince the readers about the importance of the research and the impact.

The introduction serves the purpose of giving a broad overview of the need to address a particular issue, providing a background, stating the importance or the urgency of the study, and concluding with conducting the proposed research.

A research proposal has credibility only when literature on prior research and statistical data on the topic has been cited. The review of literature will help in setting new ideas in context.

The reviewers are looking for a reason to select a few and reject hundreds of proposals. Most get rejected after reading the title and abstract.

If the reviewer reads beyond the abstract, a typing error or extra spacing is enough to be discarded. Most proposals that are not selected may not have a clear title and abstract. It is, therefore, not enough to just proofread but **get the proposal read by as many people as possible to weed out errors**.

To ensure the proposal is accepted for a Ph.D. program, researchers must ensure that the proposal is presented in a **structured manner with a flow and clarity**. Mentioning how **ethical guidelines** will be followed during the research will be advantageous. A **plagiarism check** of the draft of the proposal is a must.

If it is a group project that the proposal is being made for, **all the collaborators, experts, and affiliations** must be checked, and each of their approvals sought before submission.

Editing is an important step that includes checking for clarity in language, sentence construction, spelling, grammar, spaces, capitals, punctuation, word count, in-text citations, and references.

Before starting to write a proposal for Ph.D. research or for research funding, it is necessary to understand the scope and aims, mission, and goals of the agency to which the grants are being applied for. The checklist should help in ensuring that the proposal is not rejected. Before pressing the 'Submit' button, relook at the proposal as a reviewer, not as the researcher.

As a researcher, while you wish that the reviewers would 'trust your academic voice,' they may find some problems. This should be a great opportunity if you have to rectify the error and resubmit. Respect the reviewer's feedback comments that will help improve the proposal with a 'fresh pair of eyes!'.

Best wishes and happy researching!

I have a request for you. Please can you share your feedback by writing a short review and rate this book on Amazon.com. Your gesture will help me help other researchers better and also help other researchers seeking help in their research journey.

Thank you for your cooperation!

SUMMARY OF ALL CHAPTERS

Summaries of all the chapters are here for ready reference.

Chapter 1: INTRODUCTION

The research proposal demonstrates that you are now ready to start research by describing the plan of conducting each procedure with the timeframe for each research activity.

The literature review must show a clear need for conducting the research and how the study will add to knowledge by bridging the research gaps.

The proposal shows the researcher's understanding of the subject through the background information, identification, and statement of the problem.

The proposal must explain how it will help solve a problem or add value to what is already known.

The research proposal must be persuasive to convince the readers of the value and the research potential that the proposed work will carry. An academic research proposal must convince the reader.

Academic research work submitted as a thesis, dissertation, or project will bear the name of the institutions and universities granting the qualification.

Educational institutions and Research Centres make significant investments in building research infrastructure and resources. The research proposal must show that the resources will be utilized.

If seeking financial assistance or grants, it should show that it is worth investing in your research.

Better research preparedness will help you write the research proposal more smoothly without being constrained or feeling trapped.

Chapter 2: PREREQUISITES FOR A PROPOSAL FOR RESEARCH

Success is assured when the motivation for research, a clear goal, focus, and time are clearly defined.

Shortlist Universities where you will apply for research. Check the website for Subjects, Courses, Faculty, and their research experience, ranking, and reputation.

Look for the prescribed format on the Institution's or university website. Understanding and adhering to the guidelines laid out while writing the proposal is essential.

For a successful proposal, pre-preparations will be necessary, as will an adequate time plan.

Time and concentration are two critical ingredients to success in the research process.

Clarity, purpose, and rationale are the features common to research proposals.

Preparation in creating your personalized library by exploring databases for content online will be most beneficial.

More time will be needed to explore options if the plan is to study abroad. Before beginning to write, research and shortlist universities' websites, download their guidelines, and become acquainted with them.

Chapter 3: COMPONENTS AND STRUCTURE OF A RESEARCH PROPOSAL

Each of the components in the structure of a research proposal is important. Each component is linked to each other to bring a flow to the proposal document.

A brief introduction to your topic is sufficient for any layperson unfamiliar with the subject. The introduction may be given as a historical background or the chronological order of development. The introduction gives the context and a general overview of the topic.

The background of the study summarizes your reading of the literature on prior research and understanding of the topic. It illustrates the research done by previous researchers in the field, based on which you propose to build your research.

The review must be specific and cover all of the important ideas around the chosen research topic.

The problem statement must clearly show the gaps in research or the problem that your research seeks to resolve.

The Objectives must be specific, measurable, achievable, reliable, and time-bound. They must be defined clearly, with the main and sub-objectives, if any.

Objectives that suggest any kind of change, modification, improvement, transformation, action, or recommendations are appealing.

Hypothesis statements can be listed. Statistical analysis must be proven in support or challenged by the research results.

The research design is a plan of the procedure and sequence in which the proposed research will be conducted and comprises of the sources of data, methodology, research methods, data collection tools, sampling techniques, and so on.

Validity of results and reliability in research must be ensured.

The limitations and scope of the study are to communicate the boundaries of your research.

Chapter numbers and content must be in a logical sequence with a brief outline of each chapter.

Plan a realistic, and manageable timeframe as you will be required to submit the progress of research work on regular basis.

The conclusion can be a brief of the proposed study, from the introduction to the expected outcome of the research.

The reference list must be in alphabetical order and formatted according to guidelines.

Consider using supporting information such as developed research tools, certifications, pilot study reports, etc., as annexures to the proposal.

Once the draft research proposal is ready, you will be able to present it convincingly and be ready to start your research journey by putting the plan into action.

Chapter 4: TIPS TO MAKE YOUR PROPOSAL REJECTION FREE

Tips for developing an effective research proposal for a Ph.D. will help you with what to do and how.

Some of the best practises can be applied to any research proposal, whether to an academic institution or a funding agency.

As a researcher, you can maximize the tips listed in this chapter. Knowing what the reviewers expect helps shape the proposal so that the chances of possible rejection are minimized.

Most grants from funding agencies have strict criteria that must be understood before applying.

Researchers can use the checklist for the presentation sequence of slides in case you are shortlisted for Ph.D. admission or the research grant.

Some links to samples of research proposals provided will give some ideas. But developing an effective research proposal in your style can make it stand out!

Do remember to write a review if you found this book helpful. It may take you a few minutes for you. Use the link below:

https://a.co/d/bDIPVoK

It will greatly help me and other researchers seeking help.

Thank you!

REFERENCES

1 Letter to Robert Hooke (5 Feb 1675-6). In H. W. Turnbull (ed.), *The Correspondence of Isaac Newton*, 1, 1661-1675 (1959), Vol. 1, 416. https://www.space.com/15898-isaac-newton.html

2 Grant Andrews (2017). Research Proposal: Academic Writing Guide for Graduate Students (Essay and Thesis Writing). https://www.amazon.in/Research-Proposal-Academic-Graduate-Students-ebook/dp/B073W1B2R1

3 Michele Meleen, Building Academic Writing Skills: Tips, Rules and Resources https://grammar.yourdictionary.com/style-and-usage/academic-writing-skills.html

4. How to Write an Effective Thesis Statement https://grammar.yourdictionary.com/grammar/writing/what-is-a-thesis-statement.html

5 There are Three Types of Proposal Formally. https://www.coursehero.com/file/plg01u/2-There-are-three-types-of-proposal-Formally-solicited-Informally-solicited/

6 4 Fundamental Types of Writing Styles (With Examples) https://examples.yourdictionary.com/4-fundamental-types-of-writing-styles-with-examples.html

7 Jamie Goodwin, How to Write a Proposal in 8 Steps - Professional Writing (magoosh.com) February 1, 2018 in Business Writing.

8 Building Academic Writing Skills: Tips, Rules and Resources. https://grammar.yourdictionary.com/style-and-usage/academic-writing-skills.html

8 Joel Chan, (2018) What are the best resources helpful in writing a research proposal? https://www.quora.com/profile/Joel-Chan

9 Editage Insights, PODCAST: How to write a statement of problem for your research proposal Sep 14, 2018 https://www.editage.com/insights/how-to-write-a-statement-of-problem-for-your-research-proposal

10 Haines, L. L., Light, J., O'Malley, D., and Delwiche, F. A. (2010). Information-seeking behavior of basic science

researchers: implications for library services. *Journal of the Medical Library Association: JMLA*, *98* (1), 73–81. https://doi.org/10.3163/1536-5050.98.1.019

11 Elena Golovushkina, How to Write a Successful PhD Research Proposal - PhDPortal.com

12 Morrall, R. P. (2017), Where can I find the best resources to prepare a research proposal? http://www.quora.com/What are the best resources helpful in writing a research proposal? - Quora

13 How to Write a Research Proposal https://www.birmingham.ac.uk/schools/law/courses/research/research-proposal.aspx

14 Aditya Joshi (2016) Researcher.Life 'How to Choose the Best Research Methodology for your study understand better and select.' http://ow.ly/kaLc50HsQFU

15 https://www.phdassistance.com/blog/what-is-the-major-reason-for-rejecting-a-ph-d-research-proposal-and-how-to-avoid-these-problems/

16 Top tips for researchers on how to avoid grant proposal rejection https://www.editage.com/insights/top-tips-for-researchers-on-how-to-avoid-grant-proposal-rejection

17 https://www.business-school.ed.ac.uk/sites/default/files/2018-06/How-to-Write-a-Good-Postgraduate-Research-Proposal.pdf

NOTES

NOTES

9 798890 262905

Printed by Libri Plureos GmbH in Hamburg, Germany